BOOK • VIDEO

HOT LICKS

DUKE ROBILLARD

UPTOWN BLUES, JAZZ ROCK & SWING GUITAR

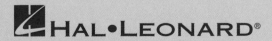

To access video visit:
www.halleonard.com/mylibrary

Enter Code
1623-8876-4248-0170

ISBN 978-1-5400-4724-3

HAL•LEONARD®

Visit Hal Leonard Online at
www.halleonard.com

Contact us:
Hal Leonard
7777 West Bluemound Road
Milwaukee, WI 53213
Email: info@halleonard.com

In Europe, contact:
Hal Leonard Europe Limited
42 Wigmore Street
Marylebone, London, W1U 2RN
Email: info@halleonardeurope.com

In Australia, contact:
Hal Leonard Australia Pty. Ltd.
4 Lentara Court
Cheltenham, Victoria, 3192 Australia
Email: info@halleonard.com.au

GUITAR NOTATION LEGEND

Guitar music can be notated three different ways: on a *musical staff*, in *tablature*, and in *rhythm slashes*.

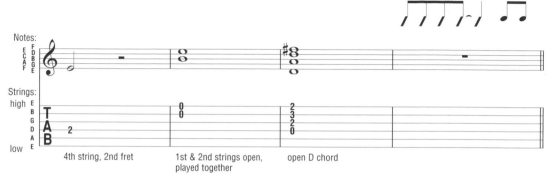

RHYTHM SLASHES are written above the staff. Strum chords in the rhythm indicated. Use the chord diagrams found at the top of the first page of the transcription for the appropriate chord voicings. Round noteheads indicate single notes.

THE MUSICAL STAFF shows pitches and rhythms and is divided by bar lines into measures. Pitches are named after the first seven letters of the alphabet.

TABLATURE graphically represents the guitar fingerboard. Each horizontal line represents a string, and each number represents a fret.

4th string, 2nd fret — *1st & 2nd strings open, played together* — *open D chord*

HALF-STEP BEND: Strike the note and bend up 1/2 step.

WHOLE-STEP BEND: Strike the note and bend up one step.

GRACE NOTE BEND: Strike the note and immediately bend up as indicated.

SLIGHT (MICROTONE) BEND: Strike the note and bend up 1/4 step.

BEND AND RELEASE: Strike the note and bend up as indicated, then release back to the original note. Only the first note is struck.

PRE-BEND: Bend the note as indicated, then strike it.

VIBRATO: The string is vibrated by rapidly bending and releasing the note with the fretting hand.

WIDE VIBRATO: The pitch is varied to a greater degree by vibrating with the fretting hand.

HAMMER-ON: Strike the first (lower) note with one finger, then sound the higher note (on the same string) with another finger by fretting it without picking.

PULL-OFF: Place both fingers on the notes to be sounded. Strike the first note and without picking, pull the finger off to sound the second (lower) note.

LEGATO SLIDE: Strike the first note and then slide the same fret-hand finger up or down to the second note. The second note is not struck.

SHIFT SLIDE: Same as legato slide, except the second note is struck.

TRILL: Very rapidly alternate between the notes indicated by continuously hammering on and pulling off.

TAPPING: Hammer ("tap") the fret indicated with the pick-hand index or middle finger and pull off to the note fretted by the fret hand.

NATURAL HARMONIC: Strike the note while the fret-hand lightly touches the string directly over the fret indicated.

PINCH HARMONIC: The note is fretted normally and a harmonic is produced by adding the edge of the thumb or the tip of the index finger of the pick hand to the normal pick attack.

PICK SCRAPE: The edge of the pick is rubbed down (or up) the string, producing a scratchy sound.

MUFFLED STRINGS: A percussive sound is produced by laying the fret hand across the string(s) without depressing, and striking them with the pick hand.

PALM MUTING: The note is partially muted by the pick hand lightly touching the string(s) just before the bridge.

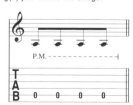

RAKE: Drag the pick across the strings indicated with a single motion.

TREMOLO PICKING: The note is picked as rapidly and continuously as possible.

VIBRATO BAR DIVE AND RETURN: The pitch of the note or chord is dropped a specified number of steps (in rhythm), then returned to the original pitch.

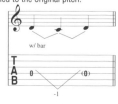

VIBRATO BAR SCOOP: Depress the bar just before striking the note, then quickly release the bar.

VIBRATO BAR DIP: Strike the note and then immediately drop a specified number of steps, then release back to the original pitch.

CONTENTS

BIOGRAPHY

In the catalog of phenomenal guitarists dotting the history of the blues, few have ever managed to display proficiency in as many diverse styles as Duke Robillard. He has made his mark on the industry as a singer, guitarist, songwriter, bandleader, and session musician.

Robillard grew up in Rhode Island, where he put together his first band while in high school. Even then he was fascinated by the connective threads between Jazz, blues, and swing music.

Robillard founded Roomful of Blues in 1967 in Westerly, Rhode Island, and remained with the seminal band until 1979. He accompanied such greats as Eddie "Cleanhead" Vinson and Big Joe Turner.

Along the way, Robillard caught the eye of Muddy Waters and jammed onstage with the legendary bluesman for several years. Robillard later signed on with rockabilly singer Robert Gordon's group and the Legendary Blues Band before founding his own group in 1981.

Originally called the Duke Robillard Band, the group, after three years of touring, became known as Duke Robillard and the Pleasure Kings. The band landed a contract with Rounder Records and released their debut in 1984, further issuing additional Rounder titles *Too Hot to Handle, Swing, Rockin' Blues,* and *You Got Me* throughout the decade of the 1980s.

In 1990, Robillard replaced Jimmie Vaughan as guitarist for the Austin-based Fabulous Thunderbirds. Four years later, Robillard signed with Point Blank/Virgin and recorded *Temptation*, followed by *Duke's Blues* (1996) and *Dangerous Place* (1997).

Robillard changed labels in 1999, moving to Shanachie, where he released *New Blues Modern Man*. This album earned him nominations for awards including Blues Band of the Year and Blues Album of the Year, as well as the title of International Guitarist of the Year from the French Blues Association. In both 2000 and 2001, Robillard was presented with the W.C. Handy Guitarist of the Year trophy.

In the following years, Robillard teamed up with guitarist Ronnie Earl to release *The Duke Meets the Earl* (Stony Plain, 2005).

As a songwriter, bandleader, and guitarist, Robillard has always explored and mastered various musical genres. Always reinventing himself and rejuvenating his musical approach, Robillard continues to tour and record, bringing his own unique take on the blues, rockabilly, Western swing, and jazz styles.

SELECTED DISCOGRAPHY

Duke Robillard

Too Hot to Handle (Rounder, 1985)

Swing (Rounder, 1988)

Rockin' Blues (Rounder, 1988)

You Got Me (Rounder, 1988)

Duke Robillard & the Pleasure Kings (Rounder, 1989)

After Hours Swing Session (Rounder, 1990)

Turn It Around (Rounder, 1990)

Temptation (Point Blank, 1994)

Duke's Blues (Point Blank, 1996)

Dangerous Place (Virgin, 1997)

Stretchin' Out [Live] (Stony Plain, 1999)

New Blues for Modern Man (Shanachie, 1999)

Conversations in Swing Guitar (Stony Plain, 1999)

Explorer (Shanachie, 2000)

Living With the Blues (Stony Plain, 2000)

More Conversations in Swing Guitar (Stony Plain, 2003)

Exalted Lover (Stony Plain, 2003)

Blue Mood: The Songs of T-Bone Walker (Stony Plain, 2004)

New Guitar Summit (Stony Plain, 2004)

The Duke Meets the Earl (Stony Plain, 2005)

Chapter 1: T-Bone Walker Style

Example 1
(1:10)

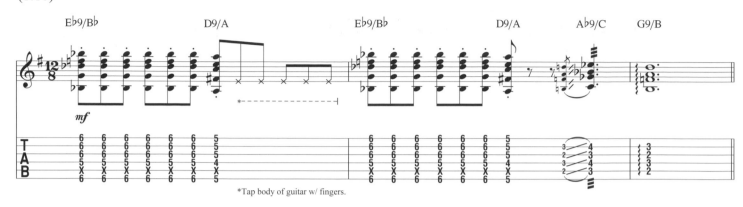

*Tap body of guitar w/ fingers.

Example 2
(1:46)

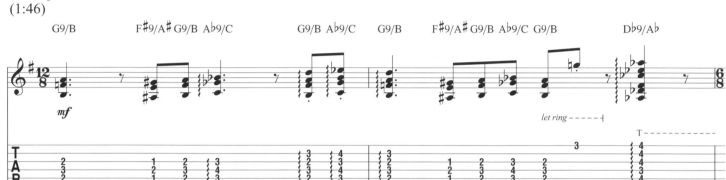

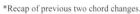

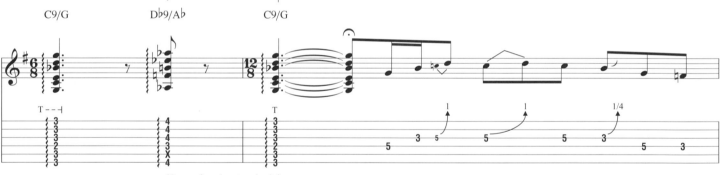

*Recap of previous two chord changes.

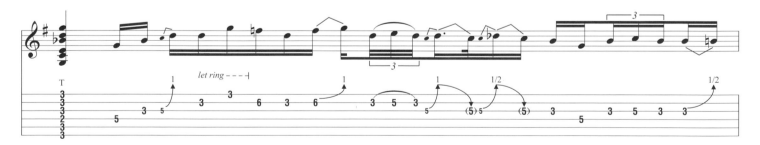

Example 3
(3:00)

Example 4
(3:33)

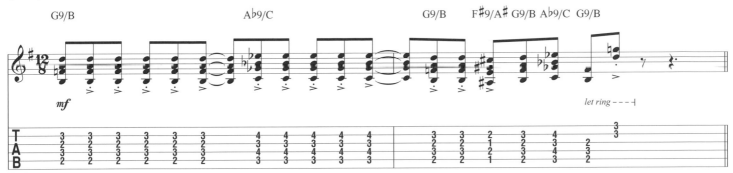

Example 5
(3:41)

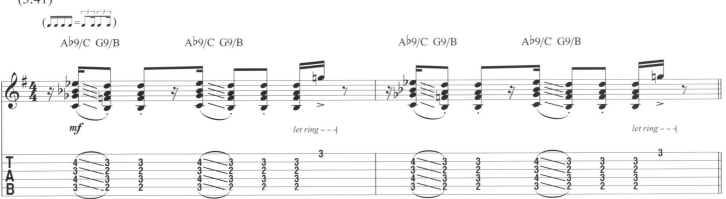

Example 6
(4:03)

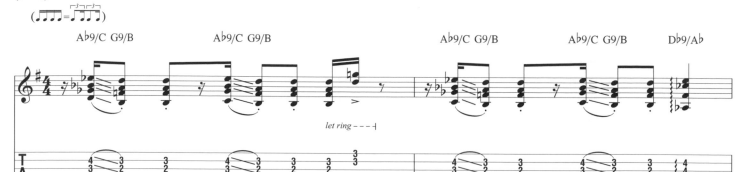

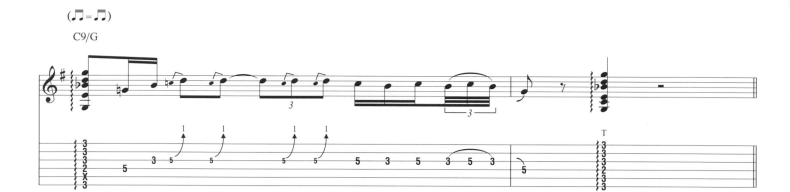

Example 7
(4:35)

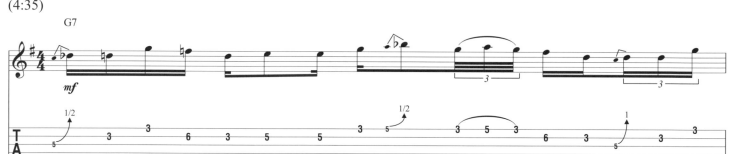

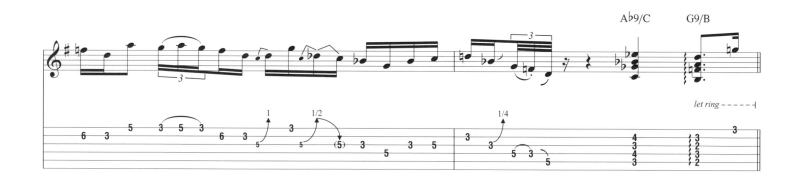

Example 8

(4:49)

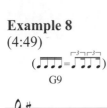

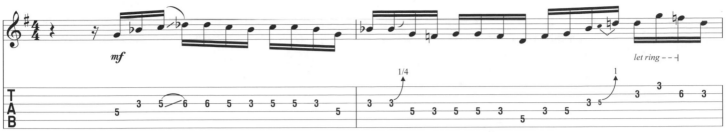

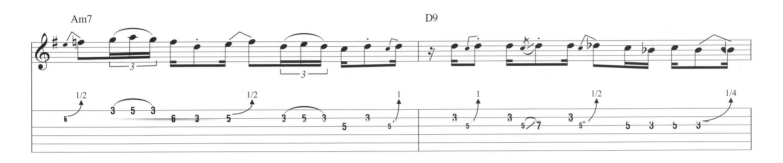

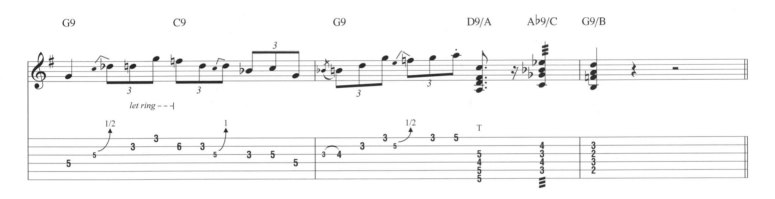

Example 9

(5:40)

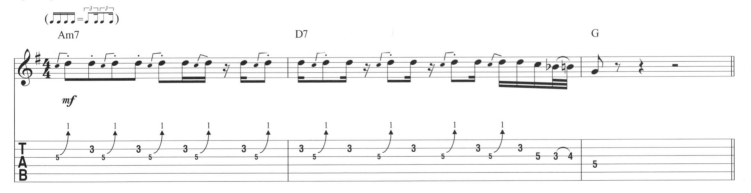

Example 10
(5:55)

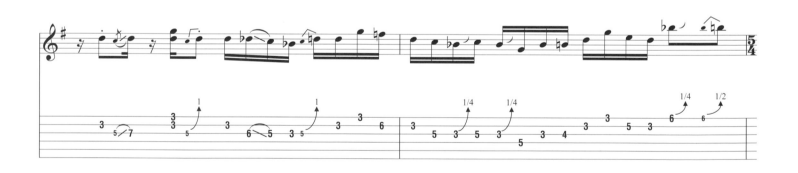

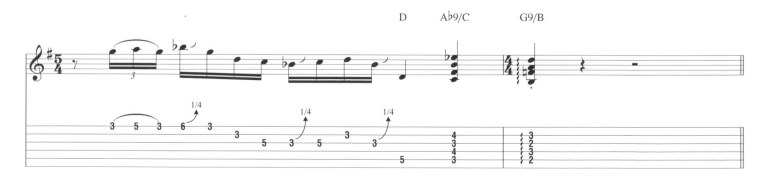

Example 11
(7:20)

Example 12
(8:15)

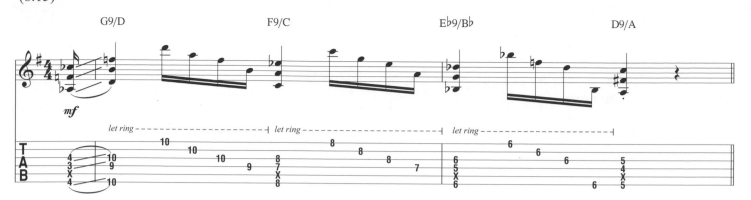

Example 13
(8:22)

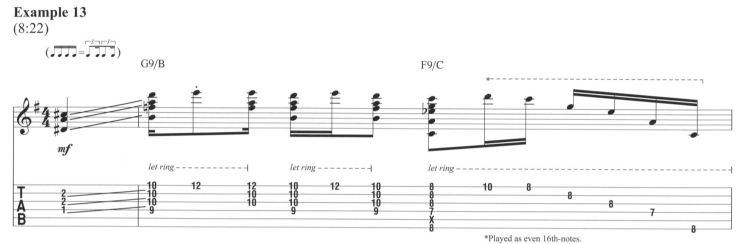

*Played as even 16th-notes.

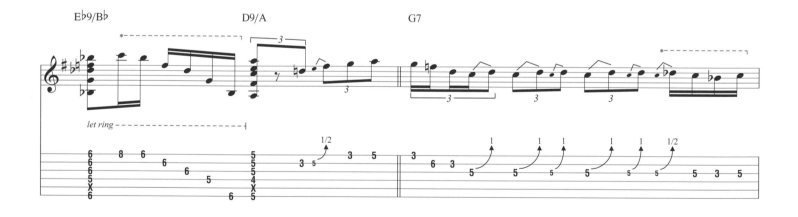

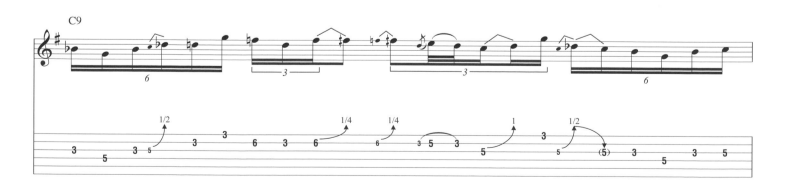

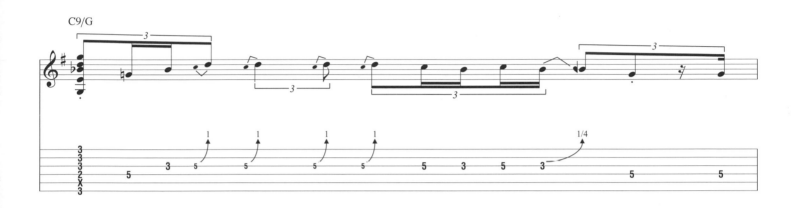

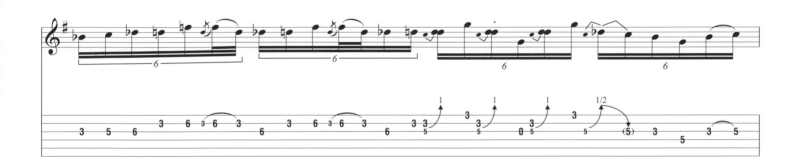

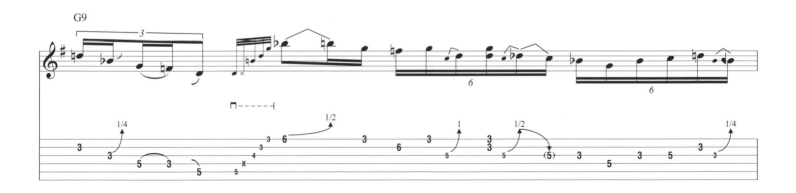

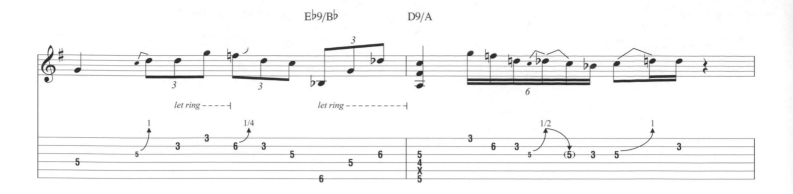

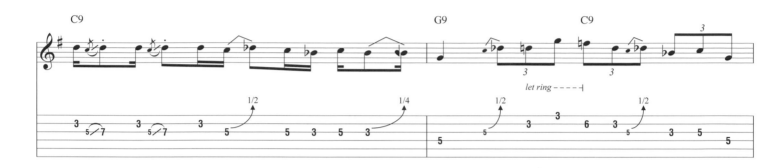

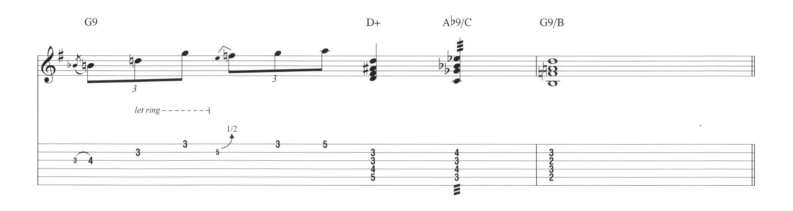

Example 14
(9:35)

Example 15
(10:17)

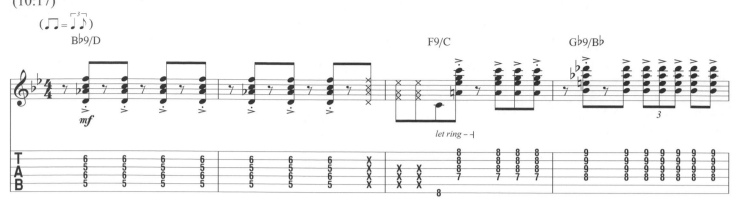

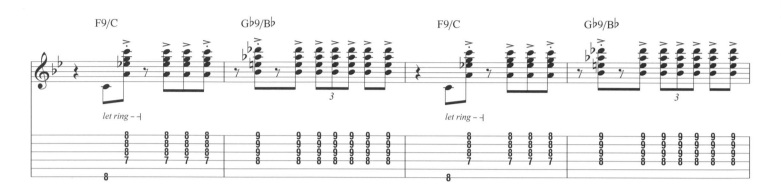

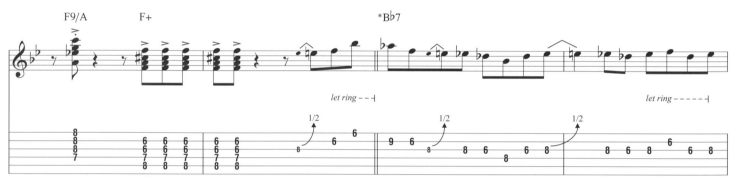

*Chord symbols reflect basic harmony.

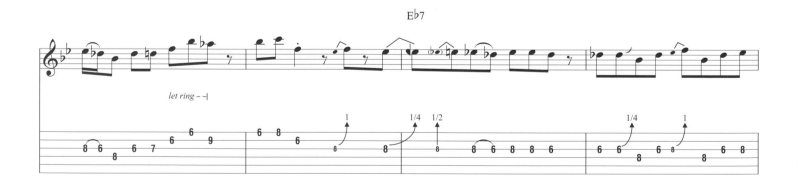

Example 16
(11:39)

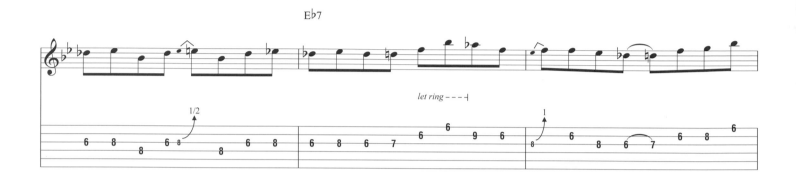

Example 17
(12:03)

Example 18
(12:29)

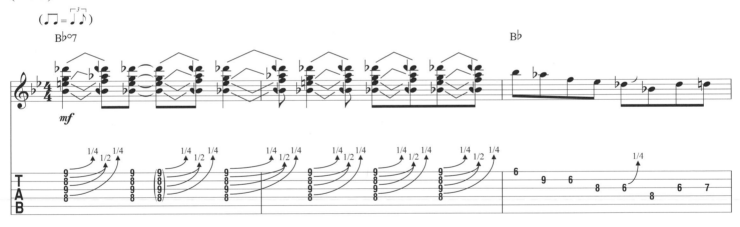

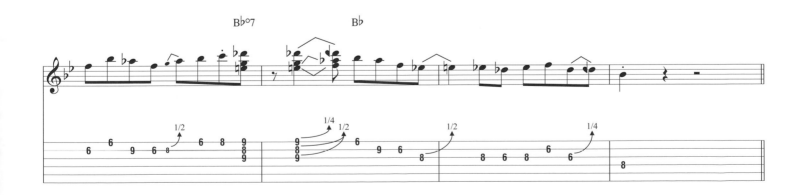

Example 19
(12:40)

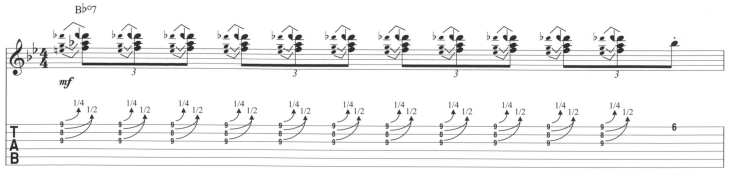

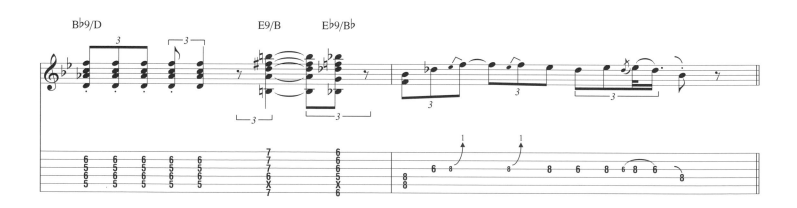

Chapter 2: Blues-Based Jazz Styles

Example 20

(:36)

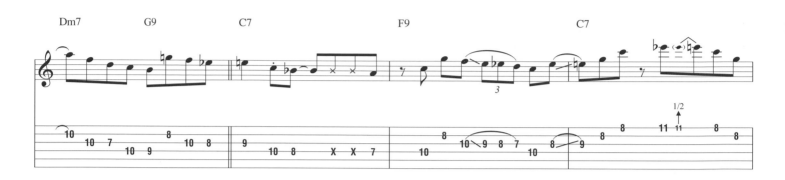

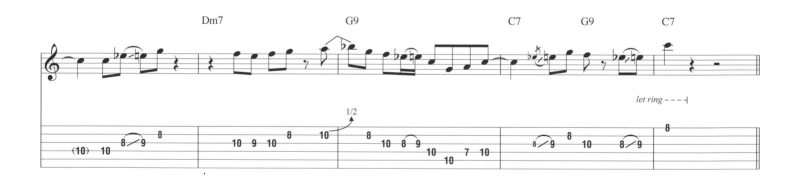

Example 21

(1:40)

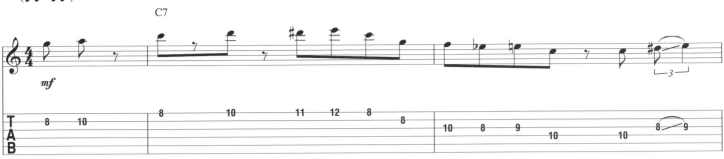

Example 22

(1:57)

Example 23
(2:40)

$(\sqcap = \overset{3}{\sqcap})$

Example 24
(3:09)

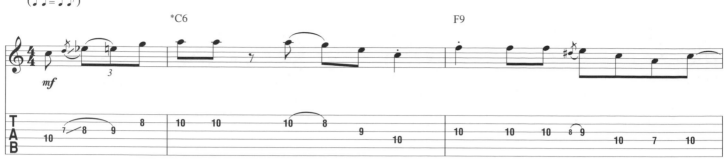

*Chord symbols reflect implied harmony.

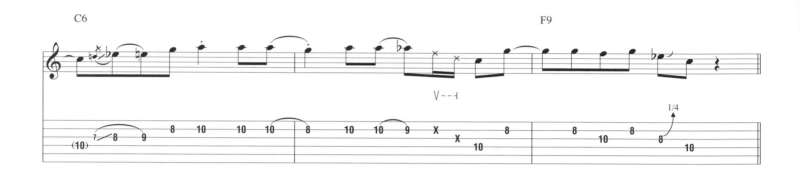

Example 25
(3:27)

Example 26
(3:48)

Example 27

(4:11)

Example 28

(4:26)

Example 29
(4:51)

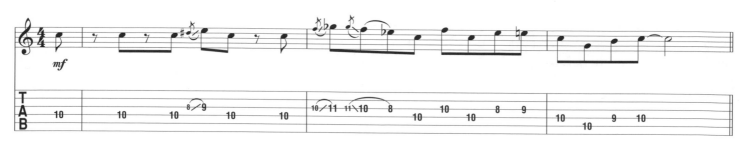

Example 30
(5:09)

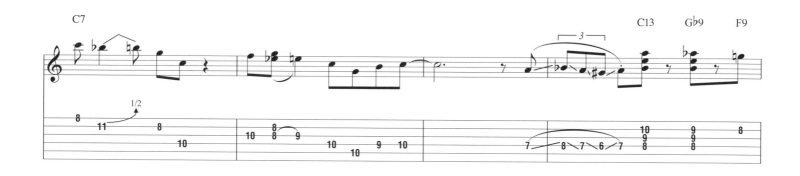

Example 31

(7:16)

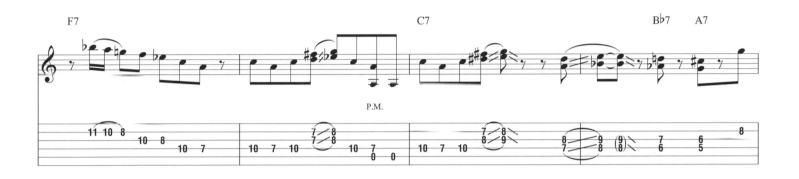

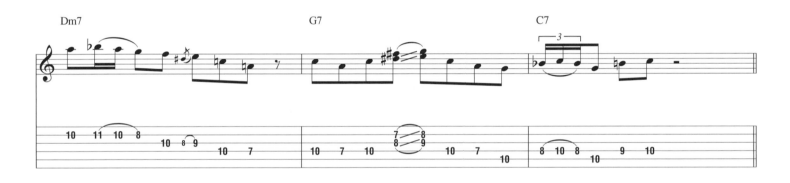

Example 32

(7:34)

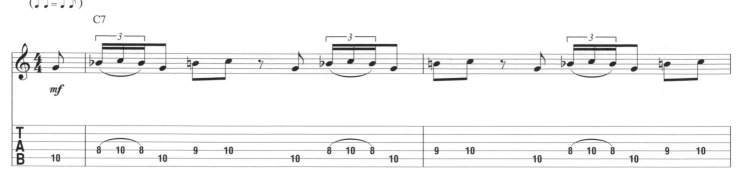

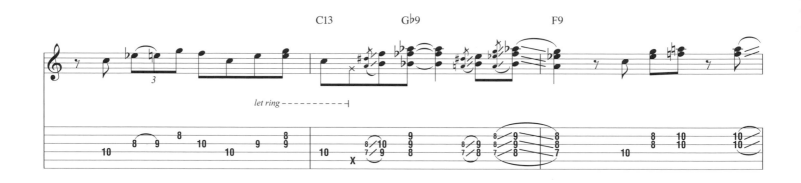

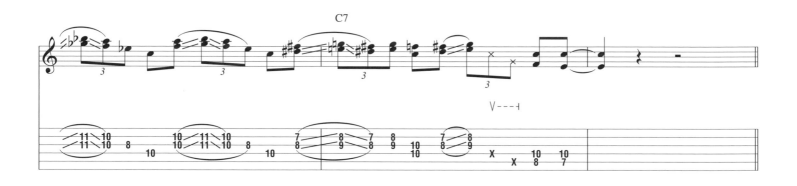

Example 33
(7:57)

Chapter 3: Les Paul Style

Example 34
(:30)

Example 35
(:57)

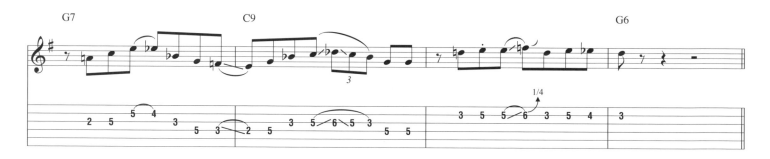

Example 36
(1:10)

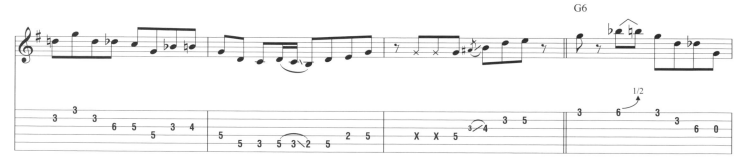

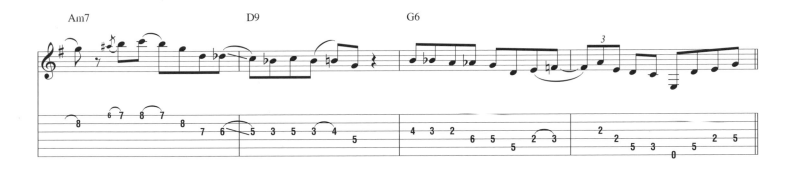

Example 37
(2:15)

Example 38
(2:49)

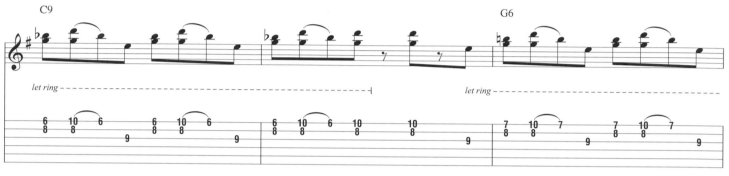

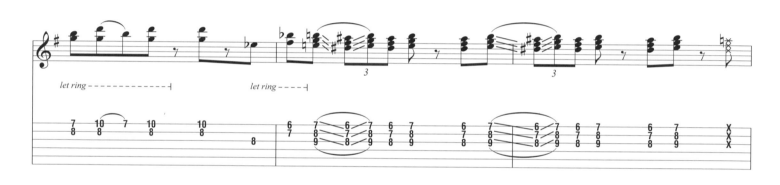

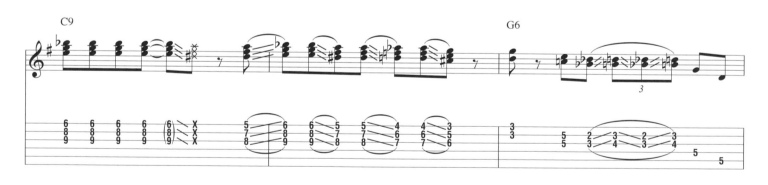

Example 39

(3:15)

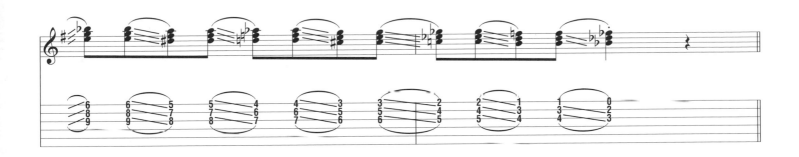

Example 40

(3:21)

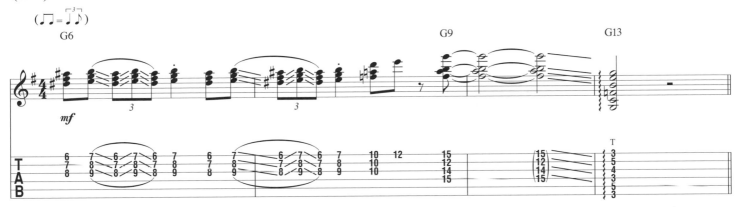

Example 41

(3:35)

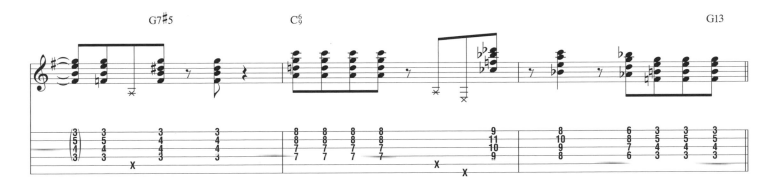

Example 42

(4:27)

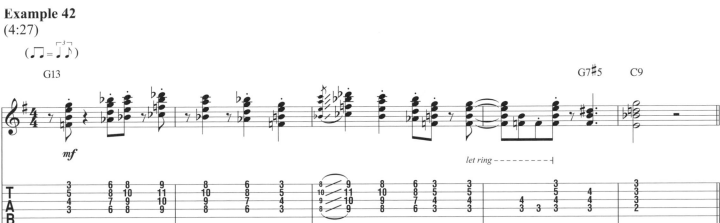

Chapter 4: Chicago Blues Style

Example 43

(:45)

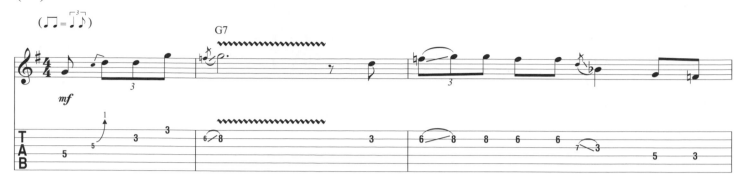

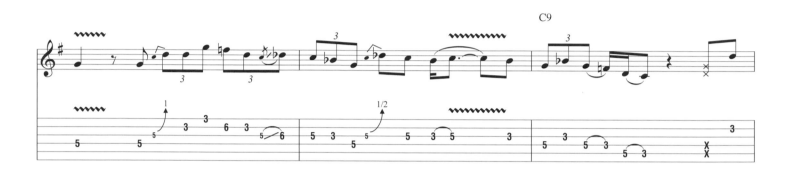

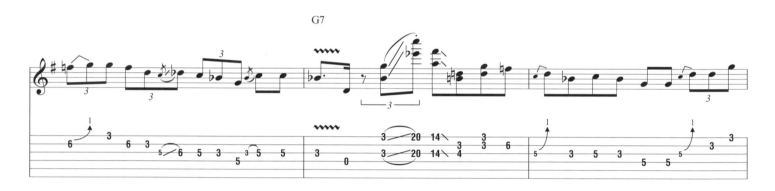

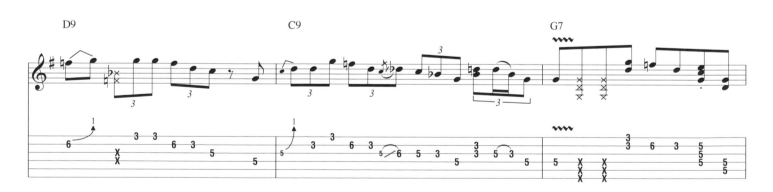

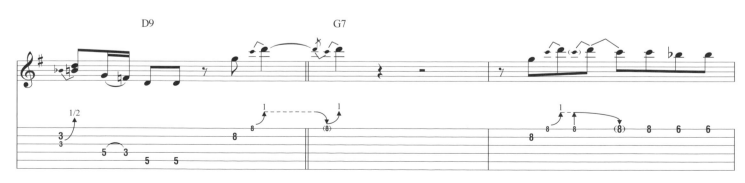

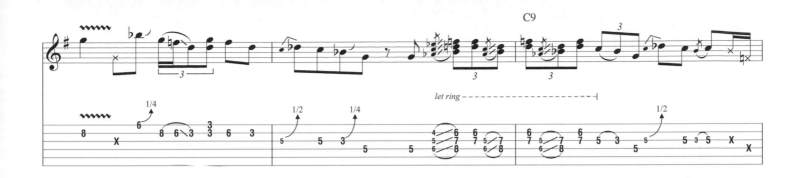

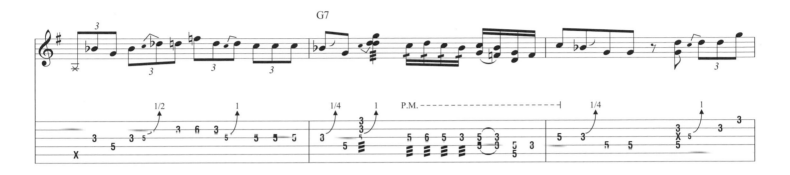

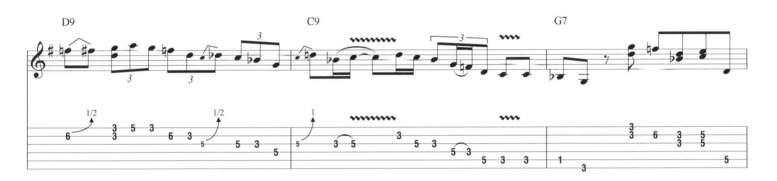

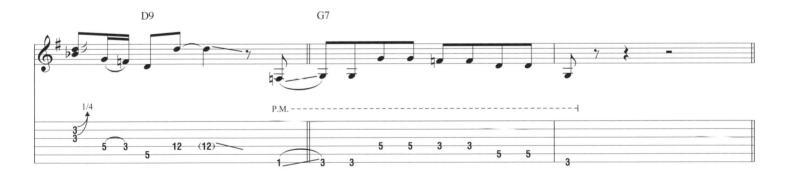

Example 44
(1:43)

Example 45
(2:17)

Example 46

(3:08)

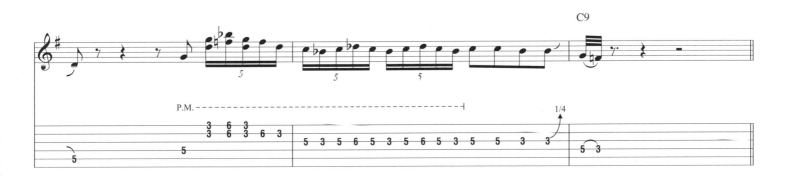

Example 47

(3:19)

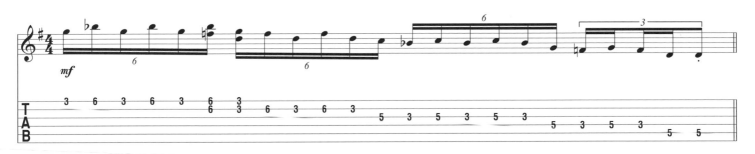

Example 48

(3:35)

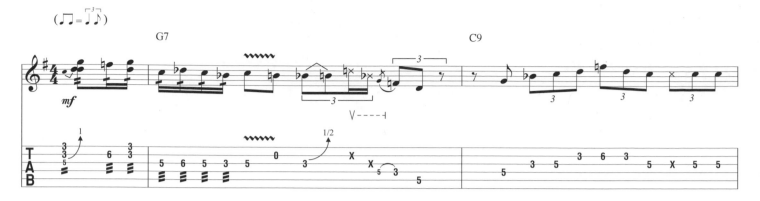

Example 49

(4:48)

Example 50
(6:37)

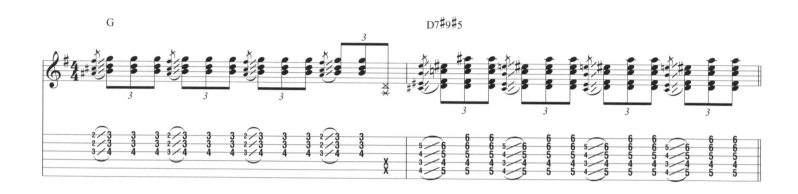

Example 51
(7:09)

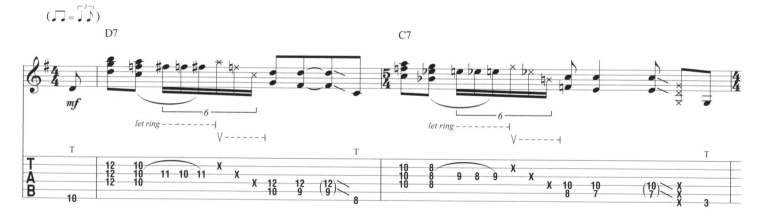

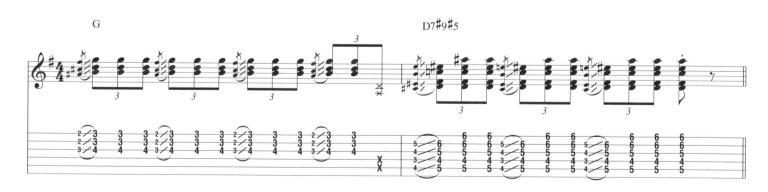

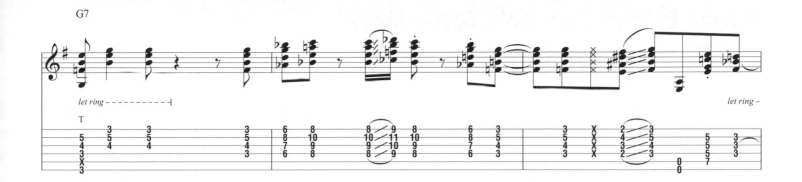

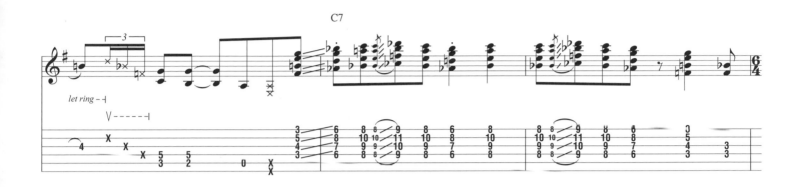

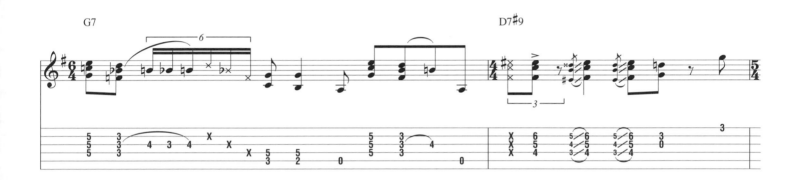

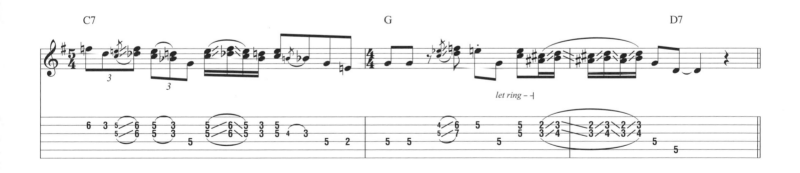

Chapter 5: Chord Fragments (Double Stops)

Example 52

(:33)

Example 53

(:49)

Example 54

(:55)

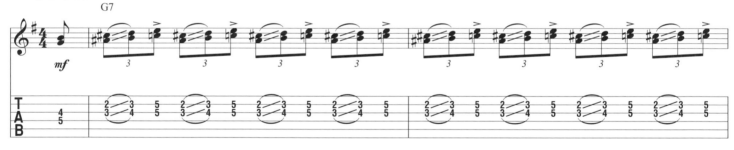

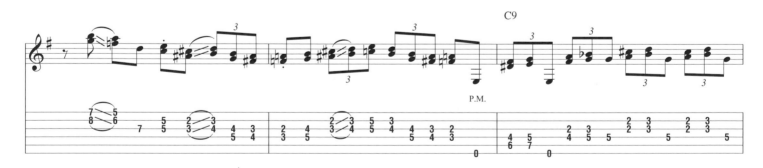

Example 55
(1:27)

Example 56
(1:51)

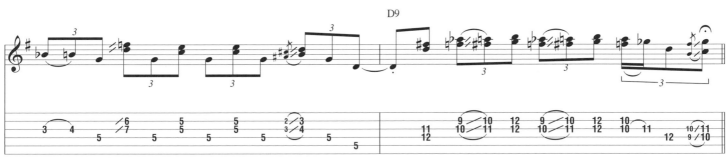

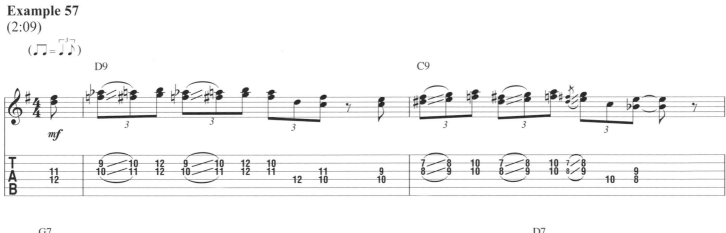

Example 57
(2:09)

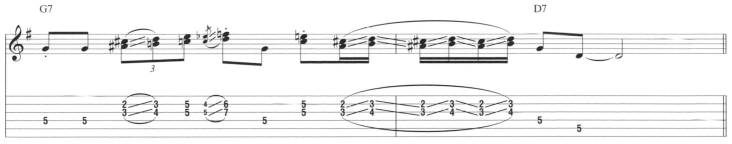

Example 58

(:48)

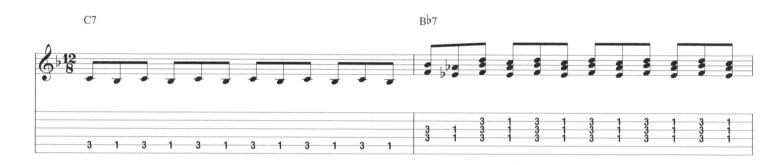

Example 59
(3:06)

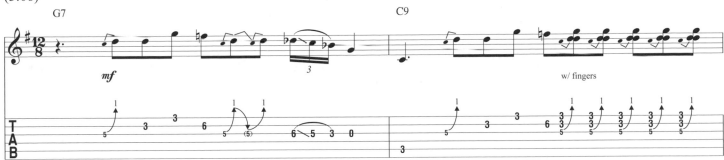

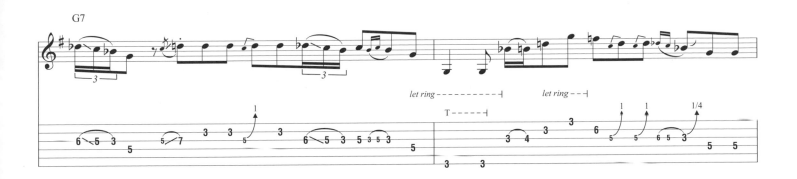

Example 60
(3:31)

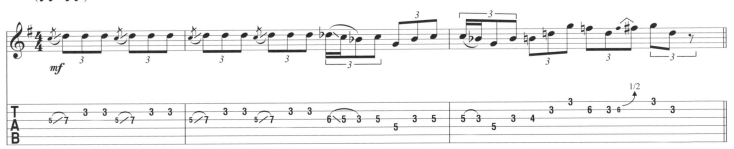

Example 61

(3:55)

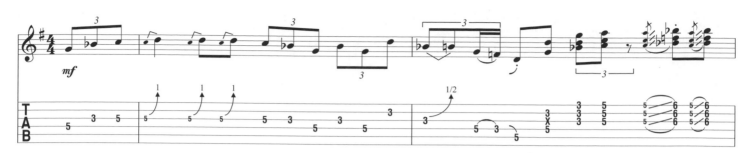

*Played as even 8th notes.

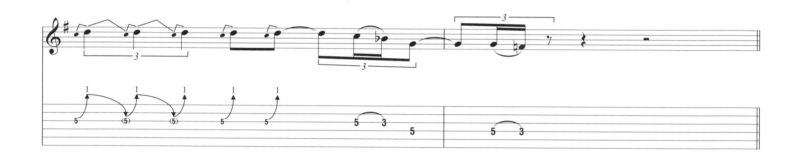

Example 62

(4:59)

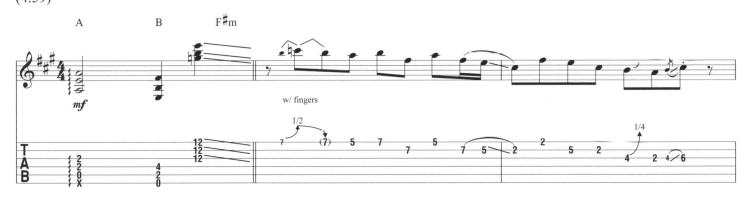

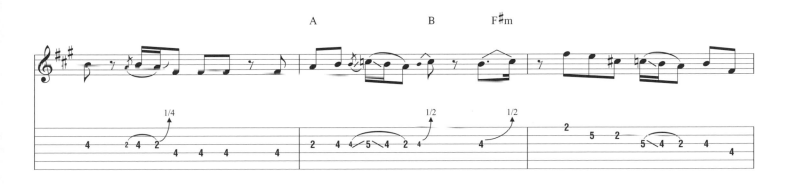

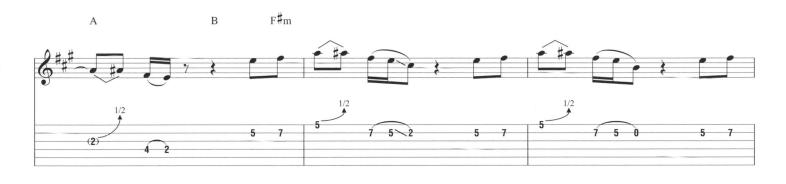

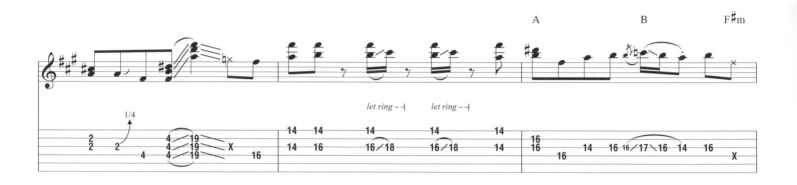

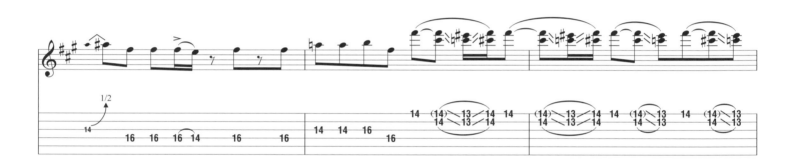

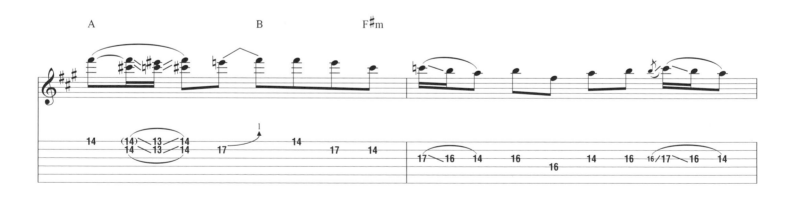

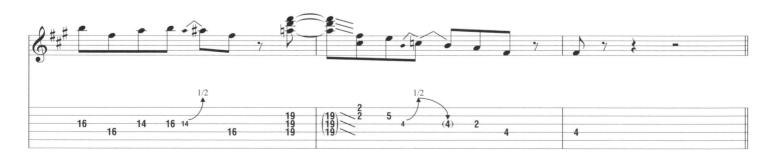

Example 63
(7:01)

F#7

Example 64
(7:28)

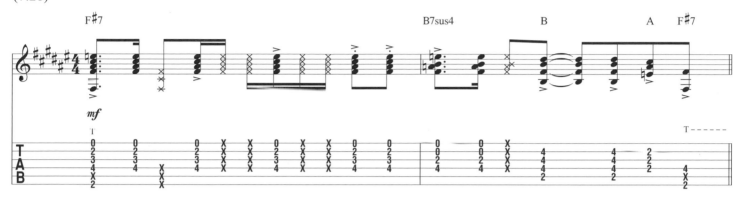

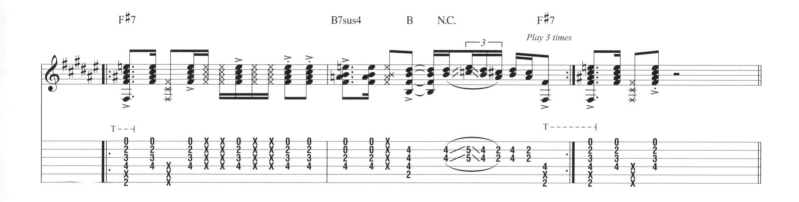

Chapter 7: Using Tremolo

Example 65

(1:10)

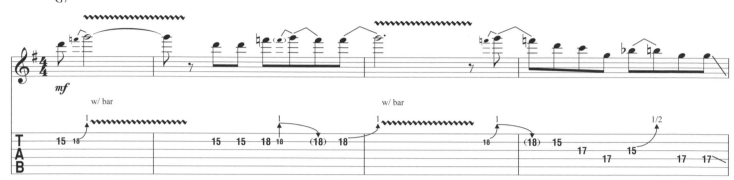

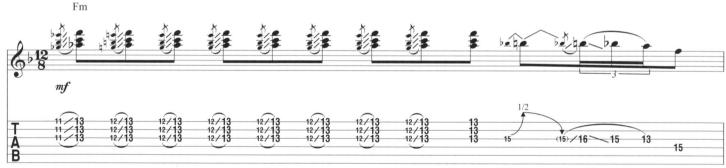

Example 66

(1:53)

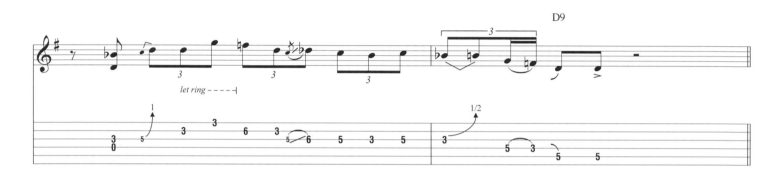

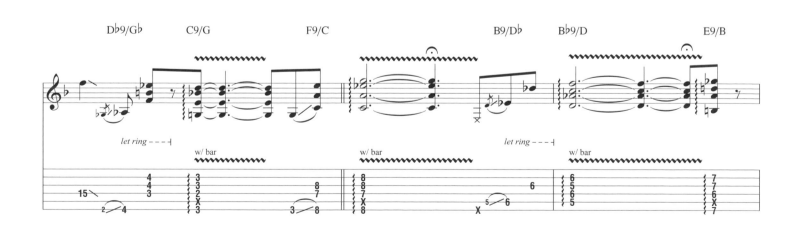

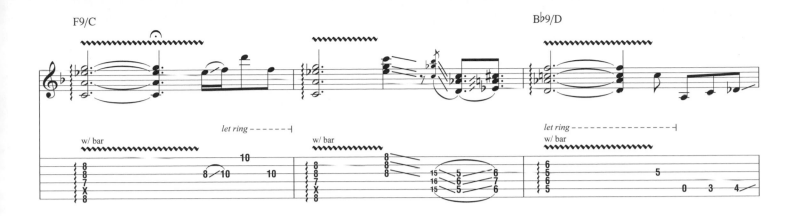

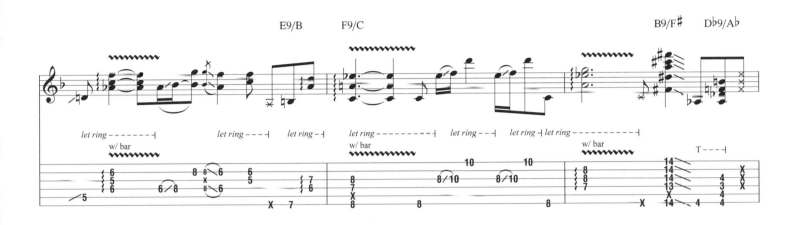

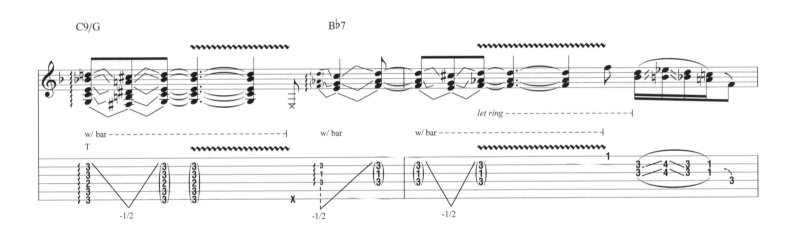

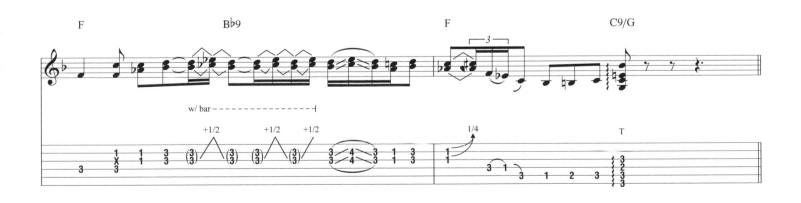

Example 67
(2:55)

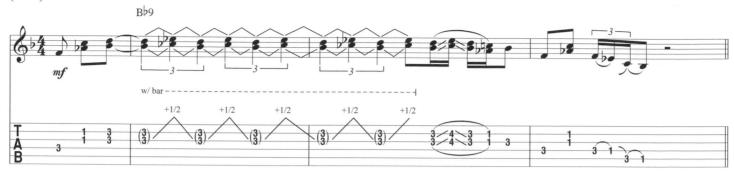

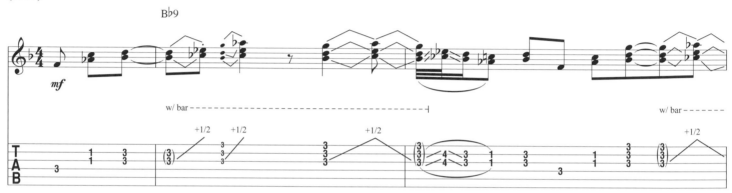

Example 68
(3:07)

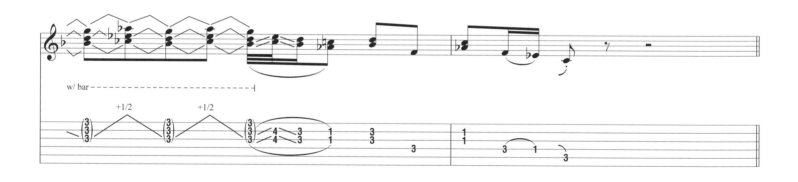

Chapter 8: Jazz Chords in the Blues

Example 69
(:01)

Example 70
(:37)

Example 71
(1:31)

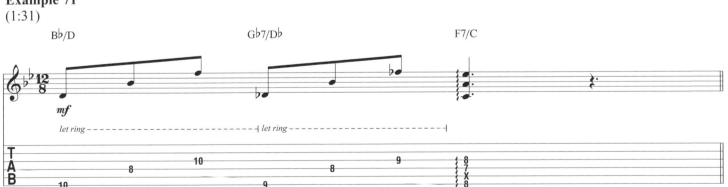

Example 72
(1:45)

Example 73
(2:27)

*T = Thumb on 6th string

Example 74

(3:33)

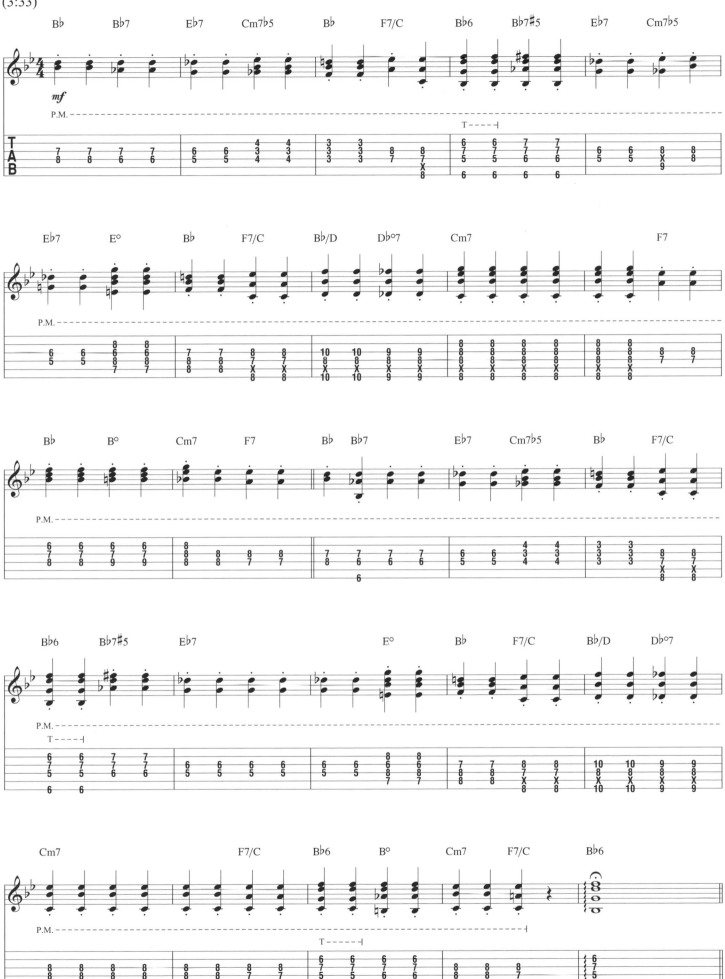

Example 75A
(4:52)

Example 75B
(5:17)

Example 75C
(5:23)

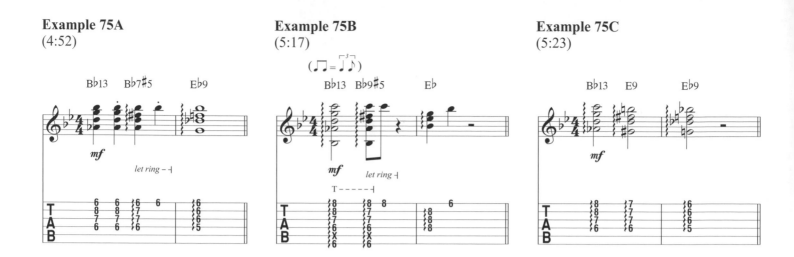

Example 76
(5:33)

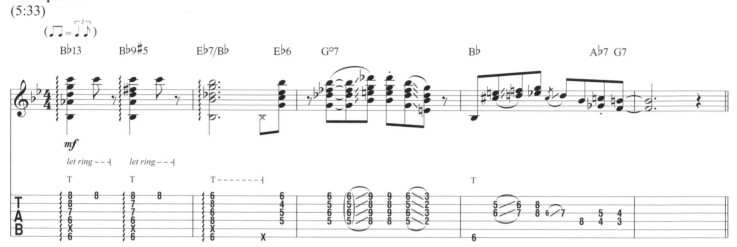

Example 77
(5:50)

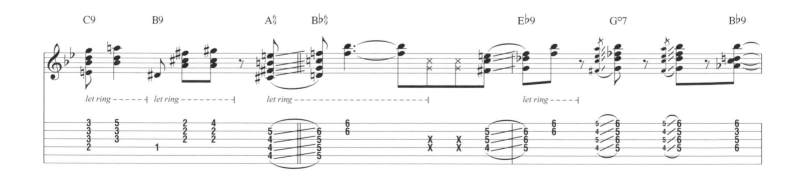

Example 78
(6:52)

HOT LICKS

For the first time, the legendary Hot Licks guitar instruction video series is being made available in book format with online access to the classic video footage. All of the guitar tab from the original video booklets has been re-transcribed and edited using modern-day technology to provide you with the most accurate transcriptions ever created for this series. Plus, we've included tab for examples that were previously not transcribed, providing you with the most comprehensive Hot Licks guitar lessons yet.

THE LEGENDARY GUITAR OF JASON BECKER
14048279 Book/Online Video..........................$19.99

GEORGE BENSON – THE ART OF JAZZ GUITAR
14048278 Book/Online Video..........................$19.99

JAMES BURTON – THE LEGENDARY GUITAR
00269774 Book/Online Video..........................$19.99

BUDDY GUY – TEACHIN' THE BLUES
00253934 Book/Online Video..........................$19.99

**WARREN HAYNES –
ELECTRIC BLUES & SLIDE GUITAR**
00261616 Book/Online Video..........................$19.99

JOHNNY HILAND – CHICKEN PICKIN' GUITAR
00289980 Book/Online Video..........................$19.99

ERIC JOHNSON – TOTAL ELECTRIC GUITAR
14048277 Book/Online Video..........................$19.99

**BRENT MASON –
NASHVILLE CHOPS & WESTERN SWING GUITAR**
14047858 Book/Online Video..........................$19.99

**DUKE ROBILLARD – UPTOWN BLUES, JAZZ ROCK &
SWING GUITAR**
00289942 Book/Online Video..........................$19.99

THE GUITAR OF BRIAN SETZER
00269775 Book/Online Video..........................$19.99

HAL•LEONARD®
Prices, contents, and availability subject to change without notice.

0719
020